The Origin and Antiquity of Freemasonry

Albert Churchward

ENTRANCE TO TATTU IN AMENTA,
SHOWING THE TWO TAT PILLARS,
RA THE GOD IN SPIRIT, AND OSIRIS WHO IS GOD IN THE BODY
OR MUMMY-FORM.
(INNERGUARD AND CANDIDATE.)

I Dedicate

this work to all my Brother Masons,

in whatever Clime and whatever Creed,

that believe in and acknowledge

the One Great Architect of the Universe.

Preface.

A T the request of several eminent members of the Brotherhood, the Author now publishes for the first time the following essay on the Origin and Antiquity of Freemasonry, the result of many years' study, labour, and research. The subject is manifestly of profound interest to the Brethren, especially to the circle of the Quator Corante, by whom these subjects are from time to time intelligently discussed. Not wishing, however, to be misunderstood, the Author admits that, so far, he has not been deemed worthy of the "Inner Circle," "The Purple," or "33°."

It is generally known that up to the present time no writer has given the true and correct origin of this wonderful Brotherhood, although many papers have been read, published, and discussed on the absorbing subject.

The Author contends that the information contained in the following pages is right and true, it having been obtained from existing facts, which can be proved by any person devoting his attention to the subject. Even to those studious persons who are not Freemasons, this information will be found to be of profound interest.

The Author has not given the whole of the passages of the different degrees, as these are secrets for the Initiated only, and because all the Brethren do not belong to the higher degrees in Freemasonry.

He has laboured to simplify the "parts of the various degrees," that it may be explicit to all who have taken them up to the 18th. At the same time the secrets are unintelligible except to those initiated; but to follow them separately and accurately one must be a 33°, as well as knowing the Egyptian Ritual or "Book of the Dead." He looks upon our present Freemasonry as a "Modernization" of the Ritual.

The Author has attained to the 18th Degree only, and could work out these absolutely perfect; there are others which he knows of from the Ritual, but is otherwise unacquainted with, not being in possession of the secrets and forms and ceremonies of the 30th, 31st, 32nd, and 33rd Degrees.

The Author is deeply indebted to the following for information, especially to his friend Gerald Massey: Le Page Renouf (the Egyptian "Book of the Dead," translated by Renouf), Dr. Le Plongeon, Mr. Marsh Adams, Brugsch Pacha, and others.

Origin and Antiquity of Freemasonry.

ANY Masons take great interest in the past history of the craft; few, we believe, have any idea of its real origin, and it is to these, therefore, more especially that this discourse is addressed. It embodies the results of many years' labours on the subject. After careful investigation of the proofs, we have brought the matter forward, feeling sure that it will be of interest to them.

All Masons who have attained to the R.A. degree must be struck by the sublime nature of its principal tenets, and, although at the present time Masonry is mainly a Brotherhood of Goodfellowship, Morality and Charity, we felt long since that it must be, so to speak, a remnant of some ancient Philosophy or Eschatology.

After long investigation we are able to throw a light on the Origin and Antiquity of Freemasonry, and proofs of the same (but we are simply dealing with its origin and antiquity, and not of the many divers and various Rituals, so called, which may have been in use for the past few hundred years), which will prove that the whole principles and tenets of the craft are the truest copy we have in existence (handed down from generation to generation) of the Eschatology of the Egyptians at the time when their Mythology and Belief were perfected in their Eschatology; and that they built the great Pyramid of Ghizeh in Egypt as a monument and lasting memorial of their religion.

Indeed, we may look on this as the first true Masonic Temple in the world, surpassing all others that have ever been built, with their secrets depicted on stone symbolically, to be read by those who have been initiated into the secrets and mysteries of their religion, after having passed through the various degrees—and it was only men (Theopneustics) of the highest honour and integrity who could possibly hope to attain to the highest or sublime degree; then only after long and patient study and many trials had been gone through to attain that end.

We do not intend to enter into any religious or theological arguments; our one object is to prove

in as compressed a work as possible, that many
of the forms, words, symbols, etc., which we. now
use were used by our ancient Brethren possibly
10,000 years ago, and that then, as now, Freemasonry
was scattered over the face of the globe, and that
the essence of their rites and beliefs was analogous
to that of our tenets; and that various pass words
were given, and had to be repeated before passing
from one degree to another, and that these were
identical with those still in use among ourselves.

Proofs of Masonry being Universal.

In 1886 Dr. Le Plongeon published a book
called "Sacred Mysteries among the Mayas and
the Quiches 11,500 years ago, and Freemasonry in
times anterior to the Temple of Solomon," and in
1896 he supplemented this with "Queen Moo and
the Egyptian Sphinx."

These books were the result of his labours
and excavations of ancient cities, etc., made in
Yucatan in Mexico, where he found many of the

signs and symbols in use amongst us. Dr. Le Plongeon is himself a Mason, and he tells us that at Uxmal he found three temples together—oblong squares—with partitions between each, and traces

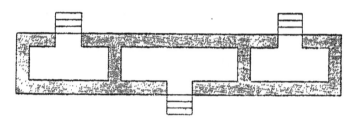

THREE TEMPLES IN UXMAL, MEXICO.

of Masonic rites in the first, second, and third degrees depicted on the walls respectively.

Most of these temples at Uxmal were surmounted by the triangular arch above a square which all R.A.M.'s will understand (the origin of which we shall have to mention hereafter).

Here we must call your particular attention to the form of the inside of the temple—a square surmounted by a triangle, with three stars in the angles of the triangle in one temple, and five

8

stars within the triangle in the other temple. As
we shall show later on, these three stars at the
corners of the triangle, with the ancient Egyptians
represented Sut, Shu, and Horus, the three Gods
of the First, or Stellar, Trinity. These, with two
others representing Osiris and Isis, completed the
family of Osiris found by Dr. Le Plongeon at
Uxmal in Yucatan.

Temple found by Dr Le Plongeon at Uxmal.

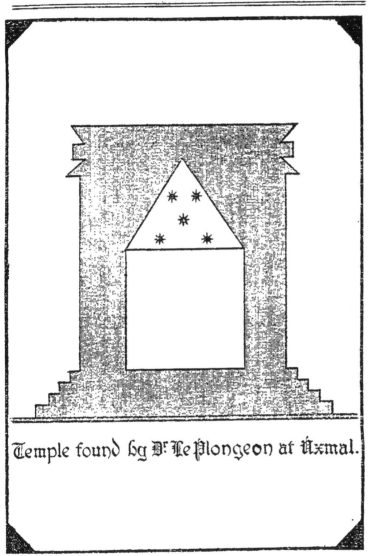

Temple found by Dr Le Plongeon at Uxmal.

Other Signs found by Dr. Le Plongeon as seen here.

1, The Emblems of Mortality; 2, The Skeleton in attitude of the Ka with upraised arms; 3, The Double Triangle; and 4, a Tau; need no explanation to R.A.M.'s.

Also the figure 5, Masonic Apron—this, evidently part of a carved statue of one of the priests. In "Dress" it is carved in white marble. 6 is from Esnè and Denderah, showing the triangle with the ✳ signs at the corners.

Some signs and symbols are likewise found in Peru among the ancient Incas, also in the mural inscriptions in the Caroline Islands, and several other Masonic signs have been met with amongst the Australian aborigines. Their form of oath is identical with that in Genesis xxiv. 9. They also name children, as Leah named her child (Gad), (Genesis xxii.), and they adopt the——in Deuteronomy xii., xiii., and xxiii.

The Masonic objects found beneath the base of the obelisk known as Cleopatra's Needle, now in the Central Park, New York, likewise show that

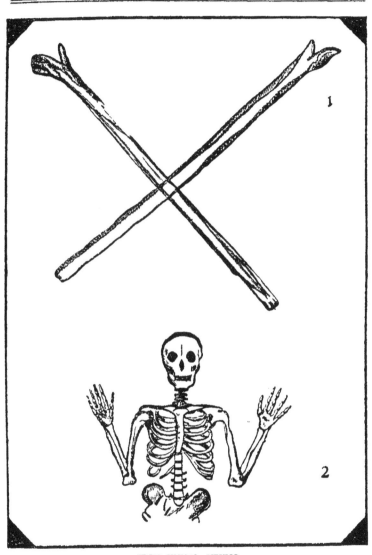

FROM UXMAL, MEXICO.

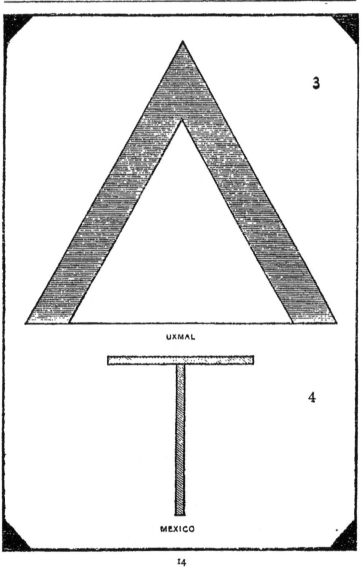

UXMAL

MEXICO

5

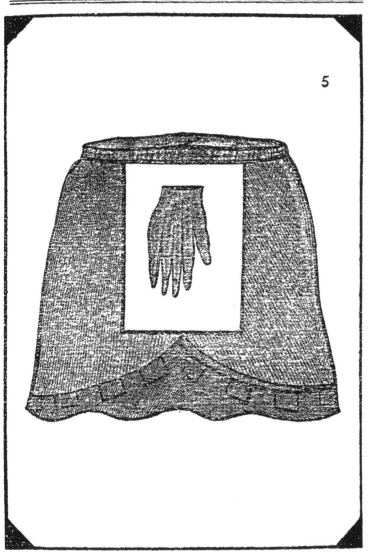

FROM UXMAL, MEXICO.

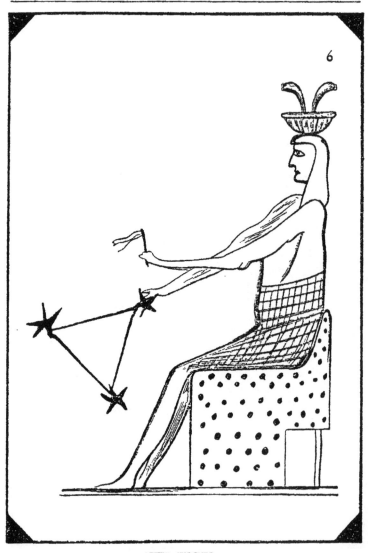

AFTER KIRCHER.

many of the symbols pertaining to the rites of modern Freemasonry were used in Egypt 3,500 years ago. This obelisk was made for Hatshepsu, who lived 1600 B.C., *i.e.* 3,500 years ago. Forbes mentions that in Java is a tribe called the Karangs, supposed to be descendants of the aborigines of the island, whose old men and youths four times a year repair secretly in procession, by paths known only to themselves, to a sacred grove in the dense forest : the old men to worship, the youths to see and learn the mysterious litany of their fathers. In this grove are the ruins of terraces laid out in quadrilateral enclosures, the boundaries of which are marked by blocks of stone laid or fixed in the ground. Here and there on the terraces are more prominent monuments, erect pillars, etc., and, especially noteworthy, *a pillar erect within a square*. Here these despised and secluded people follow the rites and customs that have descended to them through their forefathers from vastly remote antiquity, repeating with superstitious awe a litany which they do not comprehend, and whose origin and purpose are lost to their traditions, but which may be found in the Egyptian papyrus (Papyrus La of Leyden), and the Ritual or "Book of the Dead."

Gerald Massey mentions an ancient temple in North America also peculiar.

First a square within a circle, and both of them surmounted by another square; this may be said to correspond to our Quator Corante.

The Double Square or Cube.

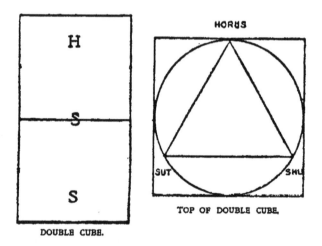

DOUBLE CUBE.

TOP OF DOUBLE CUBE.

There is an octagonal Heaven which may be formed of a double square. There were four gods

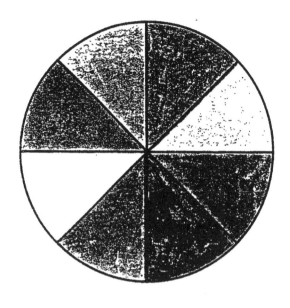

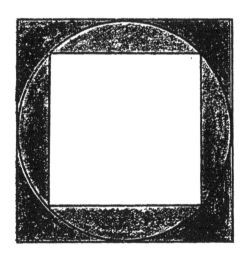

TEMPLE MENTIONED BY GERALD MASSEY, NORTH AMERICA.

of the four corners; four consorts were assigned them at the second four corners, or half-cardinal points. Twice four points are equivalent to a double square. The square may thus be doubled like the double triangle to make an octagon, as the octonary of Taht—the Moon God. The eight-fold way is equal to the square when doubled and blended in one figure.

The Japanese have an eight-forked road of Heaven.

A four-square sign 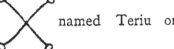 named Teriu or Khemenu, *i.e.* No. 8 is Egyptian.

4 sides of Egyptian Pyramids.

$$\frac{4 \text{ corners Assyrian Pyramids}}{8} = \text{four sides and four corners} = \text{a double square or cube.}$$

 = to a double square and circle, *i.e.*, eight half-cardinal points. Quator Corante sub-divided = to four cardinal and eight half-cardinal points. Triangle added above with three gods at the corners.

This has precisely the same meaning as the Double Triangle.

Gerald Massey is not a Mason, and we were therefore unable to learn from him if any Masonic signs existed on the walls.

We would also call your attention to these photos, one from Egypt, one from Assyria, and one from Mexico, identically the same, and identical with our P.Z. Jewels. The full explanations of these signs must be apparent to all R.A.C.'s.

The division here in twelve parts, the twelve signs of the Zodiac, = twelve tribes of Israel — twelve gates of Heaven mentioned in Revelations, and twelve entrances or portals to be passed through in the Great Pyramid, before finally reaching the highest degree.

The sign 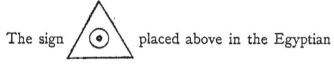 placed above in the Egyptian

and Assyrian, is well known and used by R.A.M.'s (explanation of which will be given later on), but

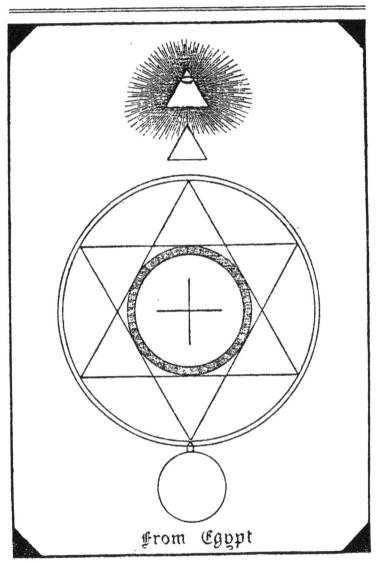

From Egypt

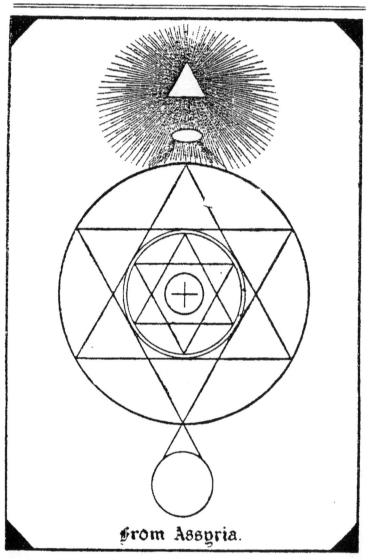

From Assyria.

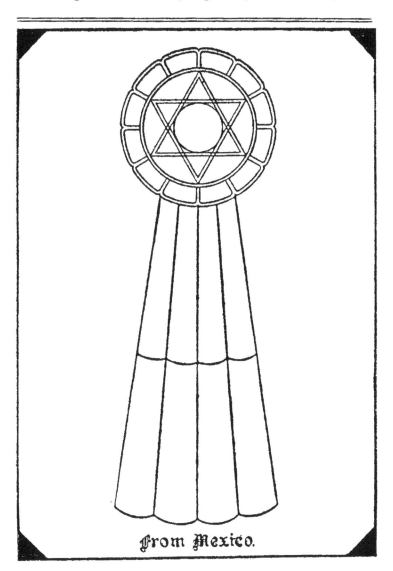

From Mexico.

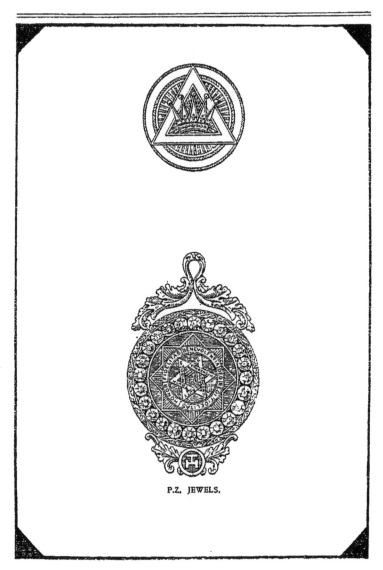

P.Z. JEWELS.

we notice the absence of this in the photograph
from Uxmal, and we have not been able to find
the sign depicted upon any of the walls or mural
carvings in Mexico.

The Origins and Explanations of other Principal Signs and Symbols used amongst us.

Take the Oblong Square first.

This sign or form was first used to represent
the Zodiac, and is found at Esnè and Denderah,
and may be considered, therefore, as the origin or
oldest form of our Lodge. (Plates may be seen in
Brugsch.)

The Square ⌐ is also very clearly depicted symbolically in the Egyptian Ritual, and is
plainly shown in the "Book of the Dead," with

25

three figures seated on it—two represented by the figure of Maat or Mati, Truth, Justice, Law, etc., the third figure being Osiris, seated on the Square in the Judgment Hall.

This Square you find depicted in many of the ancient Temples and in the Great Pyramid; as two seats, one for Osiris and one for Maat; it is the Masonic Square.

This is portrayed as the corner-stone of the Building, and the foundation of Eternal Law in the Court of Divine Justice.

The figures here exhibited are taken from the Egyptian Hall of Judgment or Righteousness. (Papyrus of Ani.)

One of these is, as you see, the great Judge Osiris, and his Judgment Seat is modelled on the Masonic Square.

Much is made in Masonry of " Acting on the Square," and here is the foundation of the whole matter.

In the Egyptian Maat, or Hall of Judgment,

MAAT OR MATI, AND OSIRIS, SEATED ON MASONIC SQUARE,
(From Papyrus of Ani.)

sits Osiris judging the dead upon the Square that is imaged by the Masonic Square, which was first employed in squaring the stones of the builders, and next in squaring the conduct in the sphere of morals of the Masonic Brotherhood, which in Egypt was as old as the Brotherhood of the seven Khemmu, or the seven Masons who assisted Ptah in building the heavens on the Square, of which the ideograph, in hieroglyphic language, is the Mason's Square.

Ptah, in Egyptian mythology, was the first great Architect of the Universe, which he built with seven assistants.

Ura [hieroglyph] Kherp Hem, who held the highest sacerdotal office in Egypt, as the High Priest of Ptah at Memphis, is also spoken of as the Arch Craftsman [hieroglyph] "tes." He raised up the body as well as the soul, and, in conjunction with [hieroglyph]

Sem and 〈hieroglyph〉 Hen nutar (prophet), exalted and anointed with oil. The Ritual says 〈hieroglyph〉. "I lustrate with water in Tattu and with oil in Abydos, exalting him who is in the heights (in excelsis)."

A great ceremony consisted in a grand procession round the walls of the Great Sanctuary of Ptah, conveying upon a sledge the "Bark" (or ark) in which the coffin of the god was supposed to rest.

The "Bark" (or ark) is that in which the soul proceeds on its journey from this sublunary abode, first from the East to the West (until Ra sets in the West). Then the soul has to disembark from this ship and has to enter, by a ladder of seven steps, another which takes the soul across the firmament, with Horus, the Son-god, at the prow, "until the stars which set in heaven are reached." (The Land of Life.) Hence the origin of the song, "To the West, to the West, to the

Land of the Free." The first "boat" (or ark) is called Mââtit—

From Photo by Emil Brugsch-Bay. Original found at Meir is now at Gizeh.
The only boat which has preserved its original rigging. Dates from 11th or 12th Dynasty.
(The dead man is sitting in his cabin wrapped in his cloak.

and the second is called Sektit in the Egyptian language. In Chapter 15 it says : " See thou Horus at the Look-out of the ship, and at his sides Thoth and Maât. All the gods are in exultation when they behold Râ coming in peace to give new life to the hearts of Chu;"—*i.e.* Horus the Son, with Truth and Justice, bringing Chu, the new-born soul, to Osiris (God), to be received by Him and all the Angels with joy and exultation into the Land of Life.

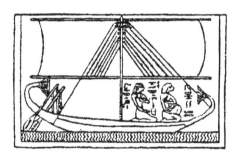

FROM BRITISH MUSEUM, No. 9,900.

The Osirian religion is at least 10,000 years old, and may be 20,000 for aught any Egyptologist knows to the contrary, but the Masonry of Ptah was indefinitely earlier than that.

Ptah was the builder who wrought in conjunction with Ma (or Mati), the Goddess of Law, Justice, Truth, etc., and we mention this to show that Ma (or Mati), was also founded on the Masonic Square.

We have no doubt our saying " To act on the Square Masonically " is from the Egyptian, " To act rightly, to act justly and truthfully, or according to Maat."

The ⌐ being the seat of Osiris in the Judgment Hall, from which place all are judged as to the past, and, before they could proceed further, must be found perfect.

Symbolically, therefore, it shows it was first, emblematically, the seat for judging right from wrong, so to speak, " To bring the material into perfect form and reject that which was not perfect."

Origin of Triangle.

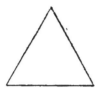

The Triangle was a primary form of the Pyramid, and a sacred symbol, because the Pyramid was typically the Pyramid of Heaven; therefore this triangle was typical of Heaven.

In the Egyptian mythology, Shu, standing on seven steps, first lifted up the heaven from the earth in the form of a triangle; and at each point was situated one of the gods, Sut, Shu, and Horus.

The Triangle, therefore, was one of the most sacred emblems; and the definition of Sut, Shu, and Horus, in Egyptian, is identical with L.A.B., as demonstrated in R.A. Chapter—the apex being at the Pole Star, where Horus, the Son, was situated.

No. 3 was a sacred number, because it represented these three which are the Trinity in its very earliest form, which was Stellar.

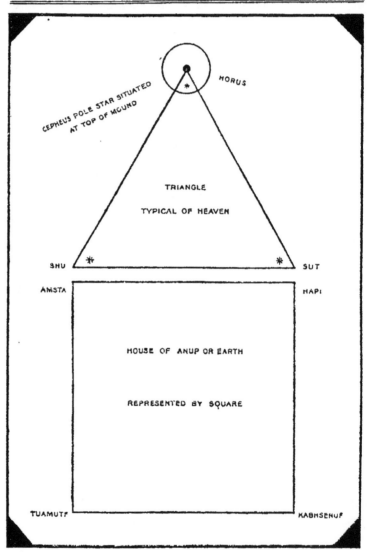

THE DOUBLE HOLY HOUSE OF ANUP.

ORIGIN OF TEMPLES FOUND BY DR. LE PLONGEON AT UXMAL

(See pages 10 and 11.)

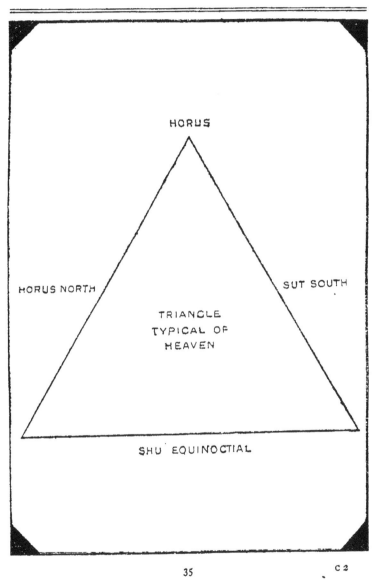

AMSTA   HAPI

HOUSE OF ANUP OR EARTH

TUAMUTF   KABHSENUF

The earth, or House of Sut Anup, was then completed by the Square, or base of Pyramid, at the four corners of which, as keepers, were the Divine Powers (the children of Horus) :—

In Egyptian : Amsta = Man.
Hapi = Lion (Ape) ⎫ *These are*
Tuamutf = Ox (Jackal) ⎭ *equivalent.*
Kabhsenuf = Eagle (Hawk).

Adapted as the signs of the four banners of the Children of Israel when they left Egypt, and the explanation of which all R.A.M.'s are well acquainted with.

Origin of the Two Columns S. and J.W.

In that beautiful Papyrus of Ani, the original of which is in the British Museum, you see the entrance to their temple depicted thus—

ENTRANCE TO TATTU IN AMENTA.

Showing the two Tat Pillars, and Ra the God in Spirit, and Osiris who is God in the Body or Mummy-form.

INNERGUARD AND CANDIDATE.

We find at the entrance two pillars. The four lines at the top represent four sides of a square (because the ancient Egyptians always drew on the flat, as they did not understand perspective), the square here representing the Terrestrial and Celestial Globes.

These pillars, which are octagonal columns ornamented, were placed at the entrance of the temple in Amenta. One was called in Egyptian, "Tat," which means in their language, "In strength"; the other "Tattu," which in Egyptian is "To establish."

The word "Tattu" also denotes the two Tat Pillars; this also means in Egyptian, "The place of establishing for ever."

The explanation of the ornamentation you see on these, is symbolically the same as the two pillars at the Porchway Entrance to King Solomon's Temple.

The Tat is a figure of stability; it supports the four corners, and is equal to the square.

Two Tats form the entrance to Tattu—a Double Square. Tattu is the entrance or gateway to the region where the mortal soul is blended with an immortal spirit, and established for ever in the mysteries of Amenta.

39

The two figures depicted here between the pillars
are, 1, Ra, the God in Spirit (Innerguard), and
2, the Spirit (Initiate) claiming entrance to
Amenta; but according to the Ritual, questions are
asked, which must be answered satisfactorily as
regards his conduct during life, before being admitted
to that immortal region, and many trials have to
be gone through and pass words to be remembered.
(See "Book of the Dead," Chapters 99 and 125.)

According to the Egyptian Creed, all these
temples were simply representatives, so to speak,
of Amenta and Heaven; their priests were human
representatives of the Divine Master, and bore
Divine titles. All these "Types" were a dual of their
belief of the same in Heaven and life hereafter;
their teachings, forms, and ceremonies, representing
their beliefs as to the life that must be led on this
earth to attain the "Throne of Glory," and the
trials the Spirit would be subject to until that was
accomplished.

" Never the Spirit was born, the Spirit will cease to be never;
   Never was time it was not: end and beginnings are dreams !
Birthless and deathless and changeless remaineth the Spirit for ever;
   Death hath not touched it at all, dead though the house of it seems."

®rigin of the Circle anð the Point within a Circle.

The Point within a circle

is one of the hieroglyphic signs of the Sun-god Ra, but it is not merely an image of the solar disc.

For one thing, it is a Masonic symbol, and H. A. Giles, the Chinese scholar, who is himself a Mason, tells us it is held to represent the one Supreme Power, whatever that power may be, the great Architect of the Universe, recognised alike by ourselves and our brother Masons of every religious denomination.*

The earliest supreme power figured in Heaven in a masculine shape, was the Power of Stability and Equilibrium, associated with the fixity of the Pole Star.

---

* H. A. Giles, "Historic China," page 389.

This was first assigned to Sut, otherwise Sut Anup, in the form of a Jackal; secondly to Ptah, the great Architect, and finally to Osiris, the power that held all things in equipoise.

The Pole Star is the first fixed point within a circle not the sun, and the earliest supreme being at the head of the seven primary stars was the god of the Pole Star.

Therefore we claim the Glyph  of Ra to have been the ideograph of the Pole Star at the centre of a circle.

And as the sceptre of Anup and the Jackal itself was assigned to the latter Solar god when he became supreme as the one who presided over the Pole of Heaven, it follows that the sign also was transferred to Ra.

The Great Architect of the Universe began to

build the House of Heaven with the Pole Star for
foundation stone, or, rather, for the coping stone
of the Cone, the Ben-ben, the House of the
Mound, when the circle was the enclosure of

Am-Khemen.

The dot in the centre of a circle is equal
to the point at the top of the cone that was
crowned with the star at the summit.

In this circle of the Pole Star there were
seven gods, or glorious ones, grouped together in
the constellation of the Lesser Bear, revolving
round the Most High, the Great Judge, the All-
Seeing Eye who saw by night, and who is the
figure of Sut-Anup at the Pole in the Planisphere
of Denderah.

The Circle of Precession takes 25,868 years to perform its cycle, and each one of the Pole Stars (7) could be seen shining down the passage opening to the north, in the interior of the Great Pyramid in its turn. (See page 65.)

The Divine Circle

became the sign of Ra in his Zodiacal Circle, but there is no such standpoint for its origin as a Solar symbol that there is for its having been the star at the centre of the Circumpolar Enclosure.

Moreover, the Glyph ⊙ is an equivalent for the Eye, and the two are co-types.

Therefore it may be inferred that as the fixed star, at the centre it was the Primordial All-Seeing Eye in the Astral mythology.

The Pole Star, considered as an eye upon the

summit of a mountain, explains the Chinese name of the "Heaven's Eye Mountain."*

The gods are described as being in their circles according to their numbers, and the god of the Polar Circle was A1, or the One, the Supreme One, and when the sign was given to Ra it denoted the One Supreme Power in his Circle, when his Circle astronomically was the Circle of the Zodiac, or eschatologically the Circle of the Universe.

The Pole being at the centre, served to determine the four quarters and the eight semi-cardinal points.

---

* De Groot. " Fêtes d'Emoui," I. 74.

Taking the sign for the Pole Star

Circle, we may infer that the wheel with eight
spokes, or the star with eight rays, is the figure
of Am-Khemen, the Paradise of the eight gods,
that is, of Sut-Anup and the seven Glorious Ones.

The sign

familiar to all R.A.M.'s, combines the enclosure of
the Pole Star with the Triangular Heaven of Sut,
Horus, and Shu.

The Triangle united to the square of the four
quarters, formed the double Holy House of Anup.
(See page 34.)

The Mountain of the Pole was the Mount of the Seven Stars, Seven Stairways, Seven Steps, and other forms of the Mythical Seven, and it is on these steps that Shu is said to have stood when he upraised the Heaven of Am-Khemen, the Paradise of the eight gods which succeeded the Circle of the Great Bear, and the Seven in the Lesser Bear.

Thus Am-Khemen was the Circle or Enclosure of the Seven, with Sut-Anup of the Pole Star, added to complete the eight.

This is the Circumpolar Paradise, upraised upon the summit of the mount that was a figure of the Pole; the Mythical Mountain of the North which was figured in the artificial Mounds, Round Hillocks, Cairns, Bee-hive Huts, Pict Houses, and other Conical Structures in all lands, and from remotest times, as burial places for the dead that were to rise again upon the Mount of Heaven.

We are unable to get back to the time when the work of the Mound Builders had no Religious or Eschatological significance.

From the first the mound of burial also denoted the Mount of Resurrection; and it is the Mount which led up to the Paradise upon the summit, first uplifted by Shu-Anhar as the Heaven of Am-Khemen.

Houses of Heaven.

When the four quarters were filled in with the twelve signs, the circle surrounding the Mount or Pillar of Earth was the Zodiac. Thus when Moses "Builded an Altar under the Mount with twelve Pillars, according to the twelve tribes of Israel" (Exodus xxiv. 4), these were an image of the Mount, and the twelve signs which marked the twelve divisions of the Celestial Circle.

This Astronomical Circle was also figured in the Hebrew Gilgal, formed with twelve pillars or stones.

Joshua is said to have taken twelve stones out of the Jordan, and set them up in Gilgal.

These were landmarks in the waters of Heaven, not in the waters of Jordan below.

The Gilgal, or circle of revolution, then was a figure of the Zodiac, and the twelve erect stones or pillars represented the twelve Celestial Signs; and an erection in the centre of this circle, a Stone, a Cairn, a Pillar, an Altar, or a Mound, would signify the Mount upon which the four supports were set up at the four cardinal points in the Circle of Heaven.

According to Muhammedan tradition, the Kaaba at Mecca had been constructed ten different times. It was first built in Heaven when the angels circled round it in procession. This shows it to have been an image of Heaven in ten different shapes, beginning with the Cone or Pyramidion of the Pole.

All ten might be made out from the figures that survive as sacred emblems, such as the Cone, Triangle, Square, Pyramid, Cube, Octagon, Cross, Circle, and the rest.

The name of the Kaaba, from Ka'ab, a cube, denotes the shape the building had assumed at the time that name was given. This would indicate the Heaven of the four quarters with Zenith and Nadir added to the Square.

Naturally the primary figure drawn in Heaven was the Circle which the Kamite record shows.

This was made definite by the turn round of the seven great stars in Ursa Major; the constellation of the Ancient Mother, also known as the Thigh=Uterus, and the Mesken, or chamber of birth.

In this circle also, turn the seven stars of the Lesser Bear (as Children of the Thigh), who represented seven primary powers here grouped together, as the seven glorious ones. They circled round the Mythical Mountain of the North, which, as a figure in Astronomy, is the Celestial Pole, and in the Eschatology, it is the Mount of Glory.

This Mount was imaged in the Conical Mound of the primeval builders.

Two figures were established as the Circle and the Cone. Thus it was seen that there was a fixed point to this Circle of the Seven Stars, determined by one never moving star, which we now call the Pole Star. This, to the earlier

Astronomers, was the star that crowned the summit of the Mount, the Cone or Pyramidion, as the fixed point in the circle of the Bears: that is, of the Great Mother and her seven children.

The Pole Star was assigned to Anup, a form of Sut, who was added to the group of seven as the eighth child of the Ancient Genetrix; who became the first or supreme one, as highest and most stable of them all, and who in the course of time was looked upon as father to the earlier seven.

The earliest fixed point within the circle was the Pole Star.

Plutarch speaks of the Egyptian Priests having a ceremony when they walk seven times around a circle, "seeking for Osiris," burning incense, resin, and myrrh. They do not find him; but Horus, the Son, whom the Ritual says has taken possession of the throne which his father has given him—he has taken possession of heaven, and inherited the earth, and neither heaven nor earth shall be taken from him, for he is Râ, the eldest of the Gods.

The Ritual mentions 10 great circles about Ra, which, with Ra's circle, would make 11; ☀ and in another part, " I travel over the earth on foot (11 to the N., 11 to the S., and 11 to the W.), returning to the E."—here was a ladder of seven steps leading to the Elysian Fields (or Heaven) (Pyramid Text, Plate 35, Papyrus of Ani)—" furnished with words of might, after encountering 'impurities and abominations' to which the damned are liable in Amenta. After I come to you, O Circle of Gods, or the Glorious and Great Ones, in Restau (or an association of persons, chiefs, princes), and bring to you N——. Grant to him bread, water, and air, and an allotment with you." Certain words of might, and the names of the Priests "who present the dead," may be given here as follows :—

𓊹𓄿𓂋𓏤𓀢 Shah-la-Mah—to salute or salaam in Egyptian. (Assyrian, Peace.) Make a peace offering.

𓅭𓏤𓄿 Se-meri-f. (Hebrew, Ab-). The Beloved

Son, or the Son he loves. Prince, Lord. The Great
One, the Mighty One, the Ever-coming One. The
Great Prince who was at the head of the seven
tribes of the Nomes or seven Astronomes in the
Heavens (*c.f.* little pigmies Stanley speaks about in
the forests of the Congo. In ancient times these
divided into seven tribes, with a Prince over each,
and one Great or Mighty One over all).

An-maut-ef may be translated, the " column "—
or support of—of the great company of the Princes.

With regard to the 10 great circles which with
" The One " made 11, and which the ancient Egyptians, according to the " Book of the Dead," believed
" that there were 10 great circles in the universe
circling around one great centre of all," making
complete the Architecture of Heaven—this must be
a different motion from the one mentioned below
—do any of our Astronomers of the present day
recognise that 10 separate divisions could be made

53

to correspond to this ? I believe not. Moreover, it would be extremely difficult, if not impossible, from observation during *one* lifetime to define these. Stellar photography has proved to us the millions of other stars that exist, which cannot be seen even with the most powerful telescope, as well as proving that constant changes are taking place, and the disintegration of the old and reforming of "new systems"; so that it would appear the ancient Egyptians could not comprehend the vastness of the universe and space, and what existed therein. All they could have done would be to mark down through 50,000 years or more that which they could see by the eye alone as far as we know.

Herodotus says the Egyptian Priests told him that they had recorded time for so long that during that period the sun had twice set where it now rises, and had twice risen where it now sets.

Drayson says the sun revolves around a centre, as we revolve around the sun, and the sun travels at the rate of 40 miles per second; therefore it would travel through space 33,000,000,000,000,000 miles *in performing its one year.* As the Priests of Egypt made observations from one generation to another, handing down in succession, each in turn, the results, the question arises, how much did they or could they map out of the universe during this period, and how much came under their observation that cannot be seen either through the telescope or from stellar photography during a period of a " present life " ?

Now let us return to Egypt, Brethren; for here, we contend, is the key and cradle of the mystery.

Disagreeing with Le Plongeon, that Yucatan was prior in its learning, and holding that the Mayas obtained their knowledge from Egypt, directly or indirectly, as well as the rest of the world, and not that the Mayas were prior in their knowledge to the Egyptians. (*Mayas*—As their traditional history shows, they certainly traded with the people of the Mediterranean, and there is reason to believe that they penetrated as far as the Himalayas.)

Everyone knows, and some of you must have

seen, that stupendous and most mysterious monument called the Great Pyramid of Ghizeh, not far from Cairo, which has been a subject of contention for years among scientific men.

The ancient name was "Khuti," which denotes the seven lights or glorious ones (see page 43), and not merely light, as Mr. Marsh Adams has stated.

This most mysterious monument stands to-day, almost perfect and intact, whilst of all other structures which made the marvels of the ancient world, scarcely a vestige remains.

But the great and grand Pyramid of Ghizeh still stands, undestroyed and indestructible, ages after the lesser marvels have passed away, as it stood ages before ever they came into existence.

Certainly more than fifty centuries, and how much more it is impossible to say for certain, have passed away since the building first concealed from view those secret chambers and hidden mysteries, of which no other building on the globe contains the equal.

What the concealed significance may be of

that secret masonry, by whom and for what purpose the complex plan was designed, has perplexed many minds and created a large amount of discord.

We maintain that the Pyramid was built at the time when the mythology of the ancient people became eschatological in its development and perfection, *i.e.*, after the Grand Master, or Priest, had received divine knowledge direct from the Grand Master above.

In its decipherment you will find the architecture of our planetary system, with their laws and movements, portrayed in minute measurements; as well as depicting their belief of Amenta.

Also in its interior is depicted hierographically and symbolically their belief as to what occurs to the departed dead before the soul is finally united to its Ka in the Grand Lodge above.

Side by side with this Masonic mystery, have come down to us various papyri of sacred writings, which have been called the Ritual of Ancient Egypt, or "The Book of the Dead," and it is to this we now turn for an explanation of the mysteries of the monument.

Not only in the Pyramid, however, were these rites and ceremonies practised and carried out, but at other Temples in Egypt—Memphis, Heliopolis, the Temple of the Sphinx; but none of these were perfect, nor did they have the whole of the symbology like the Pyramid itself, and it is only the Temple of the Pyramid and the Papyrus that show any theopneusty. A number of various Papyri that have been written at various times by different scribes have been found. We believe if we could obtain the whole "Papyri of the Pyramid" we should find a perfect ritual of the various eschatological ceremonies.

We have no doubt that a great part of the writings have been lost, but there is quite sufficient evidence extant to explain the secret.

Although the language is symbolical to a very great extent, and we have it on other evidence that the secrets of the eschatology were not written, but were declaimed and learnt orally, all that they had written being recorded in the "Pietra Libra," or Book of Stone, which the High Priests read once a year to the people.

Note to Royal Arch Masons.

The 64th Chapter and Rubric is a very important one to all R.A.M.'s. It commences with "I am Yesterday, To-day, and To-morrow (Alpha and Omega)," &c., and is probably the oldest of all. Two versions seem to have existed in the earliest times.

In the Rubric of one it says "This Chapter (Scroll of Papyri) was found in the City of Khemennu upon a block of Iron of the South, which had been inlaid with letters of real Lapis-lazuli, under the foot of the God during the reign of his Majesty the King of the North and of the South, Men-Kau-Ra triumphant, by the Royal Son Heru-Tă-Tă-f. triumphant. He found it when he was journeying about to make an inspection of the Temples. One Nekhit was with him, who was diligent in making him to understand it, and he brought it to the King as a wonderful object, when he saw that it was a thing of great mystery, which had never before been seen or looked upon."

In the other Rubric (Papyrus of Mes-em-neter) it says "This Chapter (Scroll of Papyri) was found or discovered in the foundation, on a Plinth, of the Shrine of the divine Hennu boat (or ark) by the Chief Mason in the time of the King of the North and of the South, Hesepti triumphant"; and it is there directed that it shall be recited by one who is ceremonially pure and clean.

This last dates B.C. 4266 and the other B.C. 3733. It is stated that it was "found." R.A.M.'s are told the present tradition.

Origin and Antiquity of Freemasonry.

All the secrets were passed on from generation to generation, and learnt by word of mouth by the priests only.

And we can only conjecture that some explanation of these secrets was written on papyrus, symbolically, so that they should not be lost for ever, at some remote period when internal changes were taking place in the country, which we read of in history, and that they might die without having transmitted them orally, being considered divine laws.

We should take up too much of your time to enter into all the details of this most interesting subject; and will now therefore draw your attention to a copy or plan, as far as is known, of the Great Pyramid, if you will consider that you have the Ritual, or "Book of the Dead," in your hand.

But we must first ask you to try and understand that the Ritual, or "Book of the Dead," is what is written and known as their religious belief, as far as their writings have been discovered. Our opinion is, the "Book of the Dead" contains a true decipherment of the symbolic language found depicted in stone in the Pyramid itself, teaching their belief as to what occurred to the spirit after leaving the body, and what it had to pass through before it could reach the Grand Lodge above, and thus pointing out, and laying down, a guide to our thought and actions while in this sublunary abode; also in Amenta; so that the departed soul might be able to pass through the various ordeals encountered hereafter, namely, by learning to obey the principles of Truth, Justice, and Morality in this life.

In Chapter 15, Hymn 3, of the " Book of the Dead," it says : " Freedom for ever from perdition is derived through this Book, and upon it I firmly take my stand."

In the double symbolism of Pyramid and Ritual lie the chief difficulties of decipherment, and the strongest evidence of their correspondence.

For as the departed in his progress was ultimately to become united in the fulness of intimacy with the Soul of All, his Creator, so it was necessary that he should progress in the knowledge of the mysteries which envisage alike the spiritual and material creation.

To know Osiris in his forms of manifestation was the secret of power; to understand Osiris in all his names, all his places, conferred the Crown of Illumination.

But in the attainment of that knowledge there were many stages which must be traversed by the finite mortal; many grades which must be achieved by the holy departed, when the mouth of the tomb, the Portal of Eternal Day, had been opened for him, and the catechumen of divine wisdom had been adulated as the Postulant of Immortality.

The Postulant with upraised arms must be re-created in incorruption, and the soul must be born anew before the Postulant could be initiated into things divine; or, as the Ritual says: " The Ka with upraised arms is the soul to be ultimately attained by the manes perfected."

As we have it, the Initiate must pass through the fiery ordeal and be approved as adept; like Paul, who was epopt and perfect, thus showing that

Paul was a Mason and initiated into the highest degree.

The Adept must be justified in the Tribunal of Truth before he could emerge from the shadow of the halls of death, into the immediate presence of the Source of Light.

The Justified must become the Illuminate.

The Illuminate must be consummated as master, before he could obtain the innermost mansion in the divine house.

For each of such grades, according to the creed of Egypt, the Creator has assigned a distinct locality in the universe of space, and each of these localities is described symbolically in the "Book of the Dead" or Ritual, and inscribed masonically in the features and dimensions of the Pyramid.

Not to everyone, therefore, did the secrets of the Pyramid lie open, nor could there be a more unpardonable offence than the profanation of its secrets.

And as it was the character of that religion

to be concealed, and as the manifestation of the Creator is deeper and more secret yet than the knowledge of his works, so it was essential that the sacred symbols relating to Him should not betray their deepest mysteries, even to the Initiate; but should reserve their more sacred meaning for the Illuminate after full probation.

In other words, the Initiate was taught step by step, and it was pointed out to him that only by perseverance in a right and true line of conduct, could he pass to the next stage, and finally obtain the Crown of Triumph—he must lead such a life as corresponds with our tenets and teaching.

Does not this point out to us the analogy between our teachings and our own forms and ceremonies, even all the various names of the G.A.U. in each degree as we advance?

And now let me draw your attention to that map of the interior of the Great Pyramid, as well as the door of entrance.

You see that the door of entrance was placed at the north and was concealed; so that when

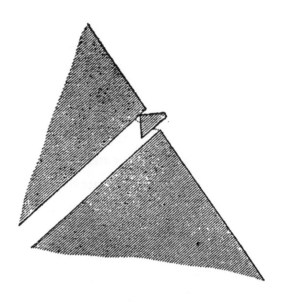

THE MOVABLE FLAGSTONE (DOOR) AT THE ENTRANCE TO THE
GREAT PYRAMID (FROM PETRIE).

looked for it could not be seen (and was only accidentally discovered).

This stone was in the form of an Equilateral Triangle, surmounting a square, and revolved on a pivot or apex.

We lay the corner stone at the north-east, and you will also perceive at this entrance you

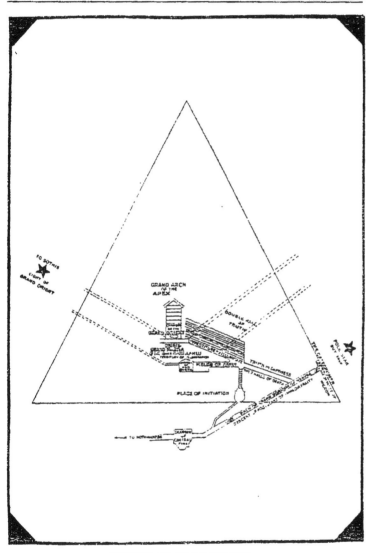

INTERIOR OF GREAT PYRAMID.

E

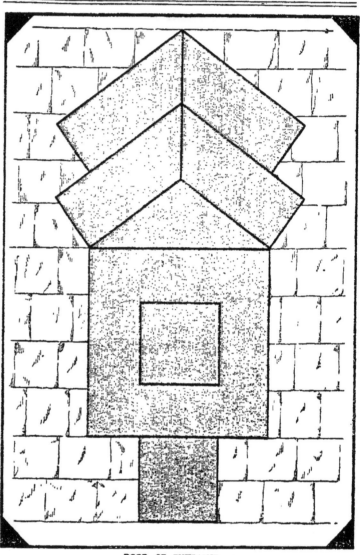

DOOR OF ENTRANCE.

have a square with a triangle above it, Typical of Heaven and Earth.

Through these the Postulant has to pass, for they symbolise the passage from this to the future life.

The Ritual shows that there were twelve entrances to pass through, before you could attain to the Grand Orient, with secrets and trials restricted to each.

The first could not be seen; it was apparently a blank and was guarded by Horus, the Son. (Innerguard.)

It was a blank or nothingness, because the Postulant was blind and bereft of all his senses except that of motion; which you see is identical with the position of our Initiate.

This portal has to be passed through with the aid of a friendly spirit.

Having passed through the portal, he is conducted down these passages by a friendly spirit, whom he cannot see; and taken to the place of initiation, where his manes is regenerated by the descent of the soul to expecting Postulants; he is then conducted to the Chamber of Central Fire, which he passes through successfully.

(You will please note that he cannot advance, as that leads to what is termed Nothingness; also, he cannot retreat, because he would not know where to go, and is blind.)

Then he is conducted up the grand horizon of Heaven, and reaches a portal; questions are asked, which he answers, and then he passes through and is able to see; light is given to him, and he can see his guide and friend who is conducting him.

In Chapter 10 of the Ritual, I.N. speaks of the desire for light, and later on " Deliver me from the Wardens of the Passages." The Wardens are the Powers who keep off the forces of the adversaries of Ra or Osiris, who sits at the head of the stairs to receive the Postulant after he has been tried in " The Tank of Flame "—which he puts out. (See Plate XI., Chapter 22, Ritual.)

He is now conducted into the Chamber of the

Shadow, Judgment of the Justified, Truth and Darkness, the Seven Halls of Death.

Here he has to pass his examination, and words are given to him which he must remember, before he is led on to the second portals, where he has to give answers also, before he can pass through them.

Having passed through the second stage, the adept is allowed to enter the hall which is called the tenth hall of Truth or Trial Scene, which is depicted by ancient brethren in black and white—the tesselated pavement, Right and Wrong, Truth or Lie—and is conducted to the Chamber of New Birth, or place of coming forth with regeneration of soul.

Here in this chamber, you will observe the emblem of mortality, the sarcophagus, empty—corresponding to our coffin.

You will also see the small opening admitting the light of that bright morning star Sothis, shining down the line into the chamber.

All the rest of the chamber reminding the

adept of what he has passed through: he now emerges from the tomb.

Then he is taken to the Throne of Regeneration of Soul, and Investiture of Illumination takes place, and then he has to pass through more ordeals to attain to the Chamber of the Orient, to the Throne of Ra, to become a Master.

The uncreated light, from which is pointed out the whole happiness of the future, he can see for himself in the distance. After passing through another portal where he has to bend, he is conducted to the Chamber of the Grand Orient.

Can anything be plainer from the brief description and passages from the Ritual I have given, than the ceremony of our entered apprentice? Passing, Raising, M.R.A., and 18°. Are these not identical? Do not the principles and tenets of the craft correspond in almost every particular? Our pass words differ somewhat, and yet the translations are symbolically almost identical. I am not giving you question and answer verbatim as they appear in the Ritual, but any brother can read them; the sense and meaning are identical with what forms our bulwark—Truth, Justice, Morality, Charity. I have, however, given you words and symbols which will be sufficient for all M.M.'s, R.A.M.'s, and others to understand the similarity of these to our own, up to and including 18°.

In the Egyptian, the word " Mati " means Law, Justice, Truth, etc. To us it teaches this lesson, that our Brotherhood will last as long as this world will last ; because we have the essence of what our Divine Creator set down as a guide for our forefathers, in the most perfect form in comparison with all others at the present time.

Our principal tenets are the same. We have a monument with the mysterious secrets written in stone which dates back to remote antiquity, and yet remains to the present day, with writing as fresh and clear as fifty centuries or more ago; and we Freemasons have practically the same signs and symbols in use now, as with the Egyptians who had the different degrees, with knowledge and secrets restricted to each, and before passing from one to another, questions and teachings had to be gone through, as well as certain ordeals to prove the faith of the brother, identical with our own.

The principles and tenets of our craft are the highest principles of Morality, Charity, Truth and Justice, which we have received as a sacred legacy from our forefathers, teaching us by sign and symbol those duties we owe to others and ourselves, to guide us through this dark life into everlasting light and happiness.

We find some of the same signs and symbols in and near the ruins of other ancient temples in Mexico and other parts of the world; and can we doubt that this, at a very remote period, was the universal belief, and these the principles practised by our forefathers?

We date our first Temple or Lodge to have been formed on the Holy Mount Moriah at the foot of Mount Horeb in the Wilderness of Sinai, with Moses A. and B. as the first G.P.'s.

At what date this occurred we have no authoritative record, and we contend that it is more than probable that if this was so, Moses became initiated into, and knew the whole of the Egyptian mysteries, and that when he left Egypt, he handed down at least some of the principles, tenets, and sacred signs and symbols to future generations; if this be so, we have it clearly in a direct line from the Egyptian originals.

No doubt much has been lost which we shall never recover; but we contend that we have shown you enough to prove that our rites and ceremonies, as well as the principal tenets of the craft, have descended from remotest ages, and that some of our signs and symbols were those used in representing the Astronomical Mythology of the Ancient Egyptians, and afterwards as sacred symbols, when the Mythology was perfected in their Eschatology; and that the G.P. was the first, and still remains the greatest, Masonic Temple in the world, open to all Masons who can read symbolically what was written in stone; ages ago, teaching the principles that we teach: that to all just, upright and true Masons there is nothing to fear, and that the Grand Master waits above ready to receive with joy the souls of those who fail not in the hour of trial.

Origin and Antiquity of Freemasonry.

Be innocent; take heed before thou act,
Nor let soft sleep upon thine eyelids fall
Ere the day's action thou hast three times scanned:
What have I done, how erred, what left unwrought?
Go through the whole account, and if the same
Be evil, chide thee; but if good, rejoice.
This do, this meditate, this ever love,
And it shall guide thee into virtue's path.